Read & Respond

FOR KS1

SECTION 1

Tyrannosaurus Drip

SECTION 2

Guided reading

SECTION 3

Shared reading

SECTION 4

Plot, character and setting

SECTION 5

Talk about it

SECTION 6

Get writing

SECTION 7

Assessment

Read & Respond

FOR KS1

Author: Sara Stanley

Development Editor: Alex Albrighton

Assistant Editor: Marion Gibson

Series Designer: Anna Oliwa

Designer: Liz Gilbert

Illustrations: David Roberts and
Andy Keylock/Beehive Illustration

Text © 2010 Sara Stanley © 2010 Scholastic Ltd

Designed using Adobe InDesign

Published by Scholastic Ltd.
Book End, Range Road,
Witney, Oxfordshire OX29 0YD
www.scholastic.co.uk

Printed by Bell & Bain

1 2 3 4 5 6 7 8 9   0 1 2 3 4 5 6 7 8 9

British Library Cataloguing-in-Publication Data
A catalogue record for this book is available from the
British Library.

ISBN 978-1407-11349-4

Acknowledgements

The publishers gratefully acknowledge permission to reproduce the following copyright material: **Macmillan Children's Books** for the use of text and illustrations from *Tyrannosaurus Drip* by Julia Donaldson, illustrated by David Roberts text © 2001, Julia Donaldson, illustrations © 2001, David Roberts (2007, Macmillan).Every effort has been made to trace copyright holders for the works reproduced in this book, and the publishers apologise for any inadvertent omissions.

Tyrannosaurus Drip

About the book

Tyrannosaurus Drip's roots lie between 'Cinderella' and 'The Ugly Duckling'. The book tells the tale of a baby dinosaur who hatches out in the wrong family. His peaceful nature and vegetarian food preferences are a puzzlement and annoyance to his adopted family, who love nothing more than meat and war and bullying the poor Duckbill to conform.

However, in the true nature of the moral tale, good triumphs over evil and the little Duckbill dinosaur relinquishes his reputation of being weak and weedy and becomes a hero! Children will also enjoy looking out for the little blue Compsognathus who starts all the trouble and watches the unfolding drama on each page.

Tyrannosaurus Drip provides numerous opportunities for children to discuss and explore the issues of bullying versus courage, aggression versus wisdom, peace versus war, the nature/nurture debate, and the habits and habitats of dinosaurs.

Children will be encouraged to enquire about identity – how we know who and what we are, and whether we should conform to peer pressure.

The book will also inspire children to use imagination and creativity to solve problems and to step into role as both hero and aggressor.

The free-flowing iambic metre of the story presents opportunities for children to experiment with pace and rhythm while enjoying the many memorable refrains. It will encourage children to further explore the many works of Julia Donaldson.

About the author

Julia Donaldson is a singer, songwriter, playwright, performer and author. She always had aspirations of becoming a poet and, as a child, wrote poems and stories on the backs of old envelopes. Her first jobs included teaching, publishing and busking around Paris and Italy performing her own songs. She also worked for many years writing songs for children's television programmes. One of her first television songs, 'A Squash and a Squeeze', was turned into a book, launching her career as an author in 1993. She has since written more than 150 books including the most famous, *The Gruffalo*.

Julia studied drama and French at Bristol University where she met her husband, Malcolm, a paediatrician who often performs with her and accompanies her on guitar. Many of Julia's books are written in rhyme, combining her love of music and poetry. Her house in Glasgow has a room full of theatrical props which are used for the stage performances of her many books.

In her spare time Julia enjoys acting, singing, playing the piano, long walks, flowers and fungi.

The illustrator, David Roberts, is a published author, editor and award-winning illustrator who has worked with a huge variety of authors. His illustrations in *Tyrannosaurus Drip* capture perfectly the characteristics and expressions of the dinosaurs, in keeping with the humour and setting of this story.

Facts and figures

Julia Donaldson has won many awards for her picture books, including the Smarties Prize and the Blue Peter Prize for the Best Book to Read Aloud for *The Gruffalo*.

David Roberts' previous work includes collaborations with his sister Lynn on retellings of several classic fairy stories. In 2006 he won the Nestlé Children's Book Prize Gold Award for his line drawings in *Mouse Noses on Toast*.

Guided reading

Introducing the book

Before breaking the story into readable chunks it is essential that the children are allowed to listen to and enjoy it. This will allow them to appreciate the sing-song rhythm and humour of the story and revel in the expressive illustrations.

During subsequent readings, reinforce and develop the children's key reading skills. Help the readers to use phonological and grammatical knowledge to decode words. Encourage appropriate pace and emphasis on rhyme. Invite children to predict key moments and ask questions to develop their understanding of the text.

The following suggestions may be used to guide and support the children's responses to the text.

Cover and title pages

Ask the children to look at the cover first of all. Highlight the wrap-around illustration and how it draws the reader to explore the blurb on the back page. Discuss the composition of the illustration and how the two Tyrannosauruses frame the title. The placement of the title draws the eye down to the hero and subject of the book: Tyrannosaurus Drip. Ask the children: *Which dinosaurs look fierce? Does the small dinosaur look frightened? What does the illustration tell us about the characters of the dinosaurs?*

Turn over to the first title page. What do the children observe? Can they begin to predict the story from the layout of the illustrations over these title pages? Point out and read the names of the author and illustrator.

Spread 1

Read the text together on both pages of this spread. Ask the children to describe the style of writing (rhyming prose) and look for the rhyming words at the end of each stanza. Allow some time to share the illustration. Ask: *How does this convey the mood of a swamp?* Discuss the illustrator's use of colour and pattern to create a peaceful, plant-like setting.

Spread 2

Before reading the text, ask the children to tell you their thoughts on the illustration. Compare the colours, atmosphere and use of fierce imagery. Note the spikiness of teeth, plants and bones compared to the swirls and soft lines.

Read the text and highlight how the author, too, has used words to create similar imagery. Which words can the children find in the text that create this fierce effect? (*Grim, grisly, mean, shouted, war* and *muttered*.)

Invite comparisons between the harshness of the word *Tyrannosaurus* with its hard 't' and the softness of the word *Duckbill* with its soft sounds.

Spread 3

Look in turn at the four illustrations across this spread. Ask the children to tell you what is happening. What do the facial expressions tell the reader about the Compsognathus's intentions and actions? Ask the children to suggest a word for each expression – for example, *sneaky, guilty* and so on.

Read the text together, placing emphasis on the rhyming words. Ask the children to predict the ending rhyme for *"Clever me!" …duckbill egg for…*

Spread 4

Were the children correct in their prediction? If so, is it spelled correctly? Ask them to explain why they think it isn't. Why is this letter typed in bold? (To highlight that the terrified Compsognathus is shouting the word.)

Point out the use of an exclamation mark to highlight the intonation and intention of surprise. You may also need to explain that the author is playing with words here and that the 'T' stands for *Tyrannosaurus*.

Read the remaining text, enjoying the rhyme and rhythm.

Encourage the children to identify the text within speech marks and demonstrate with their voices what Mother T might sound like.

Spread 5

After reading the text together, ask the children to comment on any similarities they can find in the text. Point out that Mother T's speech pattern is mirrored by that of Baby Number Three. Look at her phrase that begins, *And she grumbled…* and compare it to the baby's phrase, *And he said…* Do the children notice the sets of three words that follow the repeated statements? Point out the repeated use of Mother T's 'w' words, (*weedy, weak*) and the baby's 's' words (*sorry, simply*).

Spread 6

Look together at the illustration across this double-page spread. Ask: *How does the illustration show the difference between the two breeds of dinosaur?* Draw the children's attention to the light beam that surrounds and highlights the little Duckbill dinosaur. This is an example of symbolism where light equals goodness.

Read the text together and ask the children to provide examples of any patterns of language they have already encountered in the book – for example, *And they shouted…* and *For he hooted…*

Spread 7

Before reading the text, ask the children to comment on the illustration. What do they think is happening and why? Encourage observations that the illustration of Drip is in isolation, surrounded only by text.

Ask the children: *How do you think Drip is feeling?* Invite them to show this using appropriate expression in their voices as they read his speech.

Spread 8

Read the text and ask the children to think about times when they have discovered they could do something new, as Drip does here. Now ask them to use their imaginations to think about what they would like to suddenly discover they could do and to explain why.

Spread 9

Ask the children to comment on what it is that Drip sees in the water. (His reflection.) Challenge them to suggest other surfaces or materials that they might see their reflection in. Record some words that describe what a reflection might look like.

Spread 10

Look closely at the illustration on this spread. What are the children's first thoughts about the contrast between this page and the previous one? Discuss the colours and shadows. Which specific images does the illustrator use to convey the mood of the text? (The volcanoes erupting, swirling seas, dark skies and lightning.)

Spread 11

After reading the text, challenge the children to suggest descriptive words to describe a water monster. Point out that Drip has no shadowy reflection in the water. Why do they think this is? Discuss whether the reflections are imagery for the dinosaur's scary personalities.

Spread 12

What expressions do the Tyrannosaurus parents use to show that they do not believe there are scary monsters? Ask the children to give examples of exclamations people make when they are told about or see something strange. Encourage them to explain the meaning of the word *scoffed*. Can they think of a word meaning the opposite which could describe the next illustration of the father T jumping in the air?

Guided reading

Spread 13

Invite the children to read this spread quietly or silently first. Now ask them what they notice about the rhythm of this text. Can they identify how the rhythm has changed? Ask the children to clap out the six syllables in the word *Tyrannosauruses*. Allow them some time to play with all the words in the passage and put the words to a beat. How many different rhythms can they create?

Challenge the children to move or alter any of the author's words to make a different rhythm without changing the meaning.

Spreads 14 and 15

Ask the children to choose one of the Tyrannosauruses and describe the terrible journey from the waterfall to the sea. Encourage them to think about descriptive language to explain in the first person how they would be feeling as they journey down the waterfall and out to sea. Model an example, such as *I heard a loud snap...*

Ask questions, including:
- *What would they hear as they fell?*
- *How would the water feel?*
- *How would they be feeling?*
- *What movements would describe their journey?*
- *What did they pass on their journey to the sea and how did they come to a stop?*

Now ask them to look at the inside of the back cover and describe in the third person what the Tyrannosauruses might now be feeling or thinking. (*They feel...*)

Read the last page of text together. Ask: *Which sound is repeated several times in this text?* ('h') Explain that this is called alliteration and that the key word for this pattern of alliteration is *hooted*. What would happen to the rest of the sentence if the children changed the key word to *shooted*, *mooted* or *booted*? Allow some time for the children to play with the silly sounds of these new sentences.

Ask the children to think of some words that describe the final image of Tyrannosaurus Drip. Why is he called 'heroic' by the other duckbills? What makes someone a hero? Can they think of any examples of heroes and heroic acts? Did the Tyrannosauruses deserve their punishment? What do the children suggest might happen if the Tyrannosauruses return to the swamp?

Shared reading

Extract 1

● Read an enlarged copy of the extract and enjoy the rhythm and pace together.

● Ask for a volunteer to underline any adjoining words that start with the same sound. (*Rushy river*, *duckbill dinosaur*, *grim* and *grisly*, *two Tyrannosauruses*.) Explain that this is called alliteration. Can the children offer any of their own examples of alliteration?

● Ask the children to circle all the punctuation in the text. What do they notice about the way the text is punctuated? Note how few full stops there are and how many commas. This is because the text has to flow.

● Look at the exclamation marks and ask the children to tell you what they are used for. What is an exclamation? Ask for examples of exclamations and notice what happens to the speaker's voice. Read the phrases with exclamation marks. Now remove them and see how it alters the reader's voice.

Extract 2

● Read the first half of the extract together. Which word is repeated frequently in this passage? (*Little.*)

● What happens if you substitute the word *little* with the word *big*? Note that the two syllables of *little* create a sing-song effect.

● Ask the children to highlight any rhyming words in this first section. Do the rhymes have the same spelling endings? Note that *eggs* has a different spelling to *legs*.

● Now read part two of the extract. Ask the children which dominant sound they hear in this text? (The 'ee' sound.) Ask for volunteers to circle all examples of the 'ee' sound (but not necessarily the spelling). How many different ways is this sound represented? Look at the words *babies, be, T, baby, three, she, he, weedy, weak* and *beak*. List these words under the headings 'ee', 'ea', 'y', 'e' and 'ie'. Can the children think of other words they could add to these headings?

Extract 3

● Read this extract and explain that a verb is a way of describing an action.

● Ask the children to highlight examples of verbs that end in 'ed' and 'ing' – for example, *hooted, landed, spluttering, clinging* and *whooshing*.

● Read these verbs again and ask the children to tell you which are in the present (are happening now) and which are in the past tense (have already happened).

● Invite the children to transfer the tense of the 'ed' words into 'ing' words and vice versa.

● Now direct the children's attention to the word *broke*. Ask: *Is this a verb? Can it have an 'ed' or 'ing' ending added? How can we change the tense of this word?* Write up the children's suggestions on the board and discuss how this verb is formed.

● As an extra challenge, ask the children to think of some other examples of verbs that cannot change tense by the addition of an 'ed' or 'ing' ending. Create a class list.

Extract 1

Now across the rushy river, on a hill
the other side,
Lived a mean Tyrannosaurus with his
grim and grisly bride.
And they shouted, "Up with hunting!"
and they shouted, "Up with war!"
And they shouted, "Up with bellyfuls
of duckbill dinosaur!"

But the two Tyrannosauruses, so grisly,
mean and grim,
Couldn't catch the duckbill dinosaurs
because they couldn't swim.
And they muttered,
"Down with water!"
and they muttered,
"Down with wet!"
And they muttered,
"What a shame that
bridges aren't
invented yet."

Extract 2

Now the mother T had great big jaws
   and great enormous legs,
But her brain was rather little
   and she couldn't count her eggs.
And she sang, "Hatch out, my terrors,
   with your scaly little tails
And your spiky little toothies
   and your scary little nails."

Out hatched Babies One and Two,
   as perfect as could be,
But Mother T was horrified by
   Baby Number Three.
And she grumbled, "He looks weedy,"
   and she grumbled, "He looks weak."
And she grumbled, "What long arms –
   and look, his mouth is like a beak!"

Text © 2007, Julia Donaldson; illustration © 2007, David Roberts.

Extract 3

And how the duckbills hooted when he
landed with a crash,
And the tree bridge broke…

…and four
Tyrannosauruses went
SPLASH!

And spluttering, and clinging to
the branches of the tree,
They went whooshing down a waterfall
and all the way to sea.

Plot, character and setting

Descriptive dinosaurs

Objective: To identify and describe features of characters in stories, and find specific information in simple texts.
What you need: Copies of *Tyrannosaurus Drip*, large sheets of paper and pens.
Cross-curricular link: Drama.

What to do

● Ask the children to help you draw two large dinosaur shapes to represent Drip and one of the Tyrannosauruses.
● Divide the children into two groups and allocate one of the large drawings to each.
● Challenge each group to think of as many descriptive words or phrases they can to describe their dinosaurs. Encourage them to look back through the book together to find examples.

Nominate one or more children to scribe each group's suggestions onto the paper.
● Bring the two groups back together again and ask them to share their descriptive dinosaurs.
● Challenge the children in each group to demonstrate these descriptive words and phrases using movement, mime, voice or expressive gestures.
● Invite discussion and observations about similarities or differences between the two descriptions.

Differentiation
For older/more confident learners: Challenge the children to act out a descriptive word or phrase for members of the other group to guess.
For younger/less confident learners: Provide the children with an adult to scribe.

Oppositauruses!

Objective: To extend their vocabulary, exploring meanings and sounds of new words.
What you need: Copies of *Tyrannosaurus Drip*.

What to do

● Read the story and invite the children to point out any occasions where opposites are used – for example, *up/down, big/little, rolling/rest.*
● Compile a list with the children of common words that have opposites. Can the children find any good words in the book to use as examples? They might find *wet, land, rushy, mean, ran, clever, thrilled* and so on.
● Divide the children into two groups. Explain that one group are Duckbill dinosaurs and the other are the Tyrannosauruses. Sit the children in two lines facing each other.

● Each pair sitting opposite each other must now take it in turns to say either *Up with…* or *Down with…* and attach a word to this phrase.
● The opposing partners must reply *Down/up with…* and finish the phrase with the opposite of the original word.
● Continue down the line until each child has had a turn.

Differentiation
For older/more confident learners: Provide the children with paper and ask them to write their opposites. Collect the papers and re-distribute them, challenging the children to rearrange themselves so they are sitting opposite their correct oppositaurus!
For younger/less confident learners: Record a list of the suggested opposites for them to refer to. Ask the children to provide visual clues as support.

Plot, character and setting

I'd rather eat a rhyme

Objective: To listen with enjoyment and respond to stories and rhymes and make up their own rhymes.
What you need: Copies of *Tyrannosaurus Drip* and an enlarged copy of photocopiable page 15.

What to do
● Read the story, asking the children to take note of rhyming nouns. Explain that they are going to imagine that Drip will only eat food that rhymes with the food he refuses.
● Model the phrase: *Would you like some… meat? No, I'd rather have some… feet.*
● Cut out the cards from photocopiable page 15 mix them up and then place them where the children can see them.
● Ask for volunteers to come and select one card

saying, for example: *Would you like some… fruit?*
● Select another volunteer to find the corresponding rhyming card and use it to complete the answer: *No, I'd rather have a… suit.*
● Repeat until the children have found all the rhymes.

Differentiation
For older/more confident learners: Encourage the children to add an adjective to each card. For example, *Would you like some stinky meat? No I'd rather have cheesy feet.* Challenge them to think of additional rhymes and make extra cards.
For younger/less confident learners: Hand pairs of children a set of cards from the photocopiable page and ask them to work together to find the rhymes.

Compsognathus consequences

Objective: To listen to and follow instructions accurately.
What you need: Copies of *Tyrannosaurus Drip*, sheets of A4 paper folded into five sections and pens.
Cross-curricular link: Art and design.

What to do
● Read the story and look carefully at the illustrations of all the dinosaurs.
● Ask the children to describe any details they notice using adjectives – for example, *googly eyes, rectangular spots, pointy teeth.*
● Give each child a piece of paper and a pen. Ask them to place the paper vertically in front of them.
● Explain that they will be asked to draw a different part of a dinosaur in each of the five sections, but they will have to follow the instructions very carefully.
● Using examples of descriptive language and specific detail, describe a dinosaur's head that

the children should draw in the top section of their paper. They will need to leave a little indicator of where the next person should continue the drawing.
● Now ask them to fold the paper over, showing just the follow-on lines, and to pass it to the child on their right.
● Continue this process through arms and shoulders, body, legs and tail, and feet – reminding the children to leave an indicator mark each time.
● When all five sections are completed, have fun unfolding the papers to reveal a strange selection of dinosaurs.

Differentiation
For older/more confident learners: Encourage the children to take it in turns to describe the body sections using vivid visual language.
For younger/less confident learners: Split the class into groups and play the game as a collaborative activity using large sheets of paper.

Plot, character and setting

Find the egg

> **Objective:** To draw together ideas and information from across a whole text.
> **What you need:** Copies of *Tyrannosaurus Drip*, an enlarged copy of photocopiable page 16 and pens.
> **Cross-curricular link:** Geography.

What to do

● Read through the book taking note of all the different locations and geographical features – for example, the swamp, rushy river, hill, tyrannosaurus nest, broken tree bridge, volcano, waterfall and the sea.

● Display the enlarged copy of photocopiable page 16 and ask volunteers to draw each of these features in a square on the grid. (You don't need to fill all the squares. This game works best if children are limited to approximately ten guesses.)

● Model an example of how to find one of the locations using the grid coordinates. Explain that the *x* axis is stated before the *y* axis (2, b).

● Tell the children that a dinosaur egg has been hidden in one of these locations and secretly record your chosen square. The children must try to find the egg by taking it in turns to guess a square using the coordinates.

● When the egg has been found, reward the winner with a small prize and play again with the same grid, or create a new one.

> **Differentiation**
> **For older/more confident learners:** Hand each child their own copy of photocopiable page 16 to illustrate and invite them to play the game with a partner.
> **For younger/less confident learners:** Provide opportunities for children to practise using coordinates on a smaller grid before they play.

Odd one out

> **Objective:** To use talk to organise, sequence and clarify thinking, ideas, feelings and events.
> **What you need:** Copies of *Tyrannosaurus Drip* and a copy of photocopiable page 17, enlarged and cut into cards.

What to do

● Read the book and ask the children to think about the ways that Drip could be described as the odd one out. Ask questions such as: *How does he look different from the Tyrannosauruses? What differences in behaviour do you notice? What other differences are there between the two sets of dinosaurs?*

● Display the cards from photocopiable page 17 in rows, as they appear on the sheet.

● Invite the children to discuss in pairs which card in each row is the odd one out and to say why they think that. Explain that there may be more than one answer, depending on the reasoning offered.

● Encourage the pairs to share their ideas for each row with the whole group.

● Now ask the children to rearrange the cards to make new rows of three cards which could contain an odd one out and challenge the group to find one, explaining their reasons.

> **Differentiation**
> **For older/more confident learners:** Challenge them to think of their own odd ones out, listing all the similarities and differences between them.
> **For younger/less confident learners:** Start with two cards and ask the children to think what is the same and what is different about them before introducing three cards.

Plot, character and setting

Fact or fiction?

Objective: To distinguish fiction and non-fiction texts and the different purposes for reading them.
What you need: Copies of *Tyrannosaurus Drip* and a selection of non-fiction books about dinosaurs and access to websites about dinosaurs.
Cross-curricular links: ICT, science, geography.

What to do

● Remind the children that the dinosaurs in this story are fictional, but there is plenty of information available about real dinosaurs.
● Ask the children where they can find out information about dinosaurs.
● Explain to the class that they will be presenting information about the dinosaurs in *Tyrannosaurus Drip* as factual information.
● Divide the children into small groups.
● Allow time for the groups to share a selection of non-fiction books and factual websites about dinosaurs. Tell them to take note of how the facts are presented.
● Now invite the children to look through the story and identify areas of the story that they could present as fact – for example, *Some dinosaurs have red skin. Duckbill dinosaurs eat water reeds. Compsognathus dinosaurs steal eggs.*
● Bring the groups back together and invite them to share their new facts.
● Ask the children to design their own simple non-fiction books with facts and illustrations.

Differentiation
For older/more confident learners: Look at the contents page and index in non-fiction books with the children and challenge them to create their own.
For younger/less confident learners: Scribe their suggestions to create one class non-fiction book. Children can provide their own illustrations and additional notes.

Dinosaur swamp dance

Objective: To consider how mood and atmosphere are created in performance.
What you need: Copies of photocopiable page 18, pencils and a recording of Gustav Holst's *The Planets*: Mars, Venus and Mercury.
Cross-curricular link: Dance.

What to do

● Explain to the class that they will be recreating the moods and movements of the dinosaurs in *Tyrannosaurus Drip* to make a swamp dance.
● Play extracts of the three tracks and explain that they were written by Holst to convey the emotional effect and influence that the planets have on us. Don't name the tracks at this stage.
● Hand out copies of photocopiable page 18 and replay each track. Ask the children to draw the dinosaur they think represents each piece of music (Duckbill, Tyrannosaurus or Compsognathus).
● Ask the children to explain the reasons for their choices. Now tell them the title of each track and discuss whether their choices match the images of 'Mars, the Bringer of War', 'Venus, the Bringer of Peace' and 'Mercury, the Winged Messenger'. Discuss how the Compsognathus could be seen as a messenger. (He started all the trouble.)
● Using the photocopiable sheet, ask the children to draw a symbol or pattern that could describe how each dinosaur moves. Then encourage them to fill in a symbol or pattern that might describe the speed at which each dinosaur moves.
● Use the sheets as dance 'maps' to help compose a movement and rhythm for each dinosaur.

Differentiation
For older/more confident learners: Ask them to combine their work to create a longer performance piece.
For younger/less confident learners: Invite them to complete an enlarged copy of the sheet collectively.

SECTION
4

I'd rather eat a rhyme

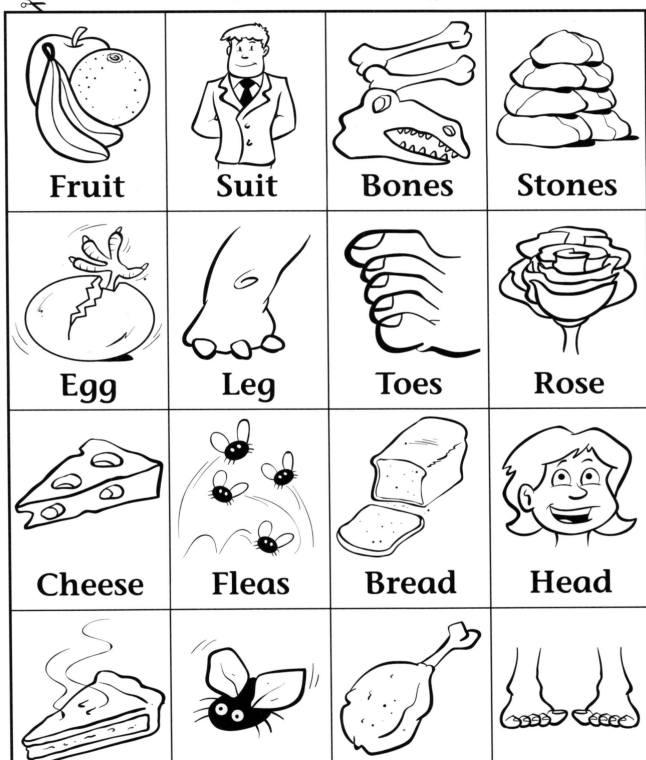

Fruit	Suit	Bones	Stones
Egg	Leg	Toes	Rose
Cheese	Fleas	Bread	Head
Pie	Fly	Meat	Feet

Illustration © 2010, Andy Keylock/Beehive Illustration.

PHOTOCOPIABLE

READ & RESPOND: Activities based on Tyrannosaurus Drip

Find the egg

● Guess coordinates to find the square where the dinosaur egg has been hidden.

	1	2	3	4	5
e					
d					
c					
b					
a					

Illustration © 2007, David Roberts.

SCHOLASTIC
www.scholastic.co.uk

READ & RESPOND: Activities based on *Tyrannosaurus Drip*

Odd one out

A volcano	**A river**	**A mountain**
A potato	**A carrot**	**A banana**
A lizard	**A crocodile**	**A fish**
A pig	**A tiger**	**A sheep**

SECTION
4

Dinosaur swamp dance

● Listen to the music and then fill in the boxes with drawings or notes to create your own dance for each dinosaur.

Title of music	Which dinosaur?	Movement symbol or pattern	Speed symbol or pattern
Mars			
Venus			
Mercury			

Talk about it

Performing dinosaurs

Objective: To explore familiar themes and characters through improvisation and role play.
What you need: Copies of *Tyrannosaurus Drip*, musical instruments, props and masks and access to video footage of Julia Donaldson reading or singing.
Cross-curricular links: Drama, music.

What to do

● Explain that Julia Donaldson often performs many of her stories and songs and that the children are going to create their own class performance of *Tyrannosaurus Drip*. You may wish to search on the internet or watch DVDs of some of her performances for inspiration.
● Divide the class into small groups and allocate each group a section of the book to work on.
● Encourage the groups to act out their part of the book – they can use sound effects or put the words to a familiar tune or rap. Invite the children to collect instruments and props that they may wish to use. You could also give them the option of drawing pictures to use as props/puppets.
● Allow time for the groups to rehearse their performances and then share everyone's work.

Differentiation
For older/more confident learners: Challenge them to make cast lists and scene titles. You could also provide recording equipment for the children to record their performance for analysis.
For younger/less confident learners: Help the children to create a role-play dinosaur swamp. Collect their suggestions for props to include.

Model dinosaurs

Objective: To ask and answer questions, make relevant contributions, offer suggestions and take turns.
What you need: Modelling material such as clay or dough and a large sheet of paper.
Cross-curricular links: PSHE/philosophy, art and design.

What to do

● Explain to the children that they are going to make a model of the best dinosaur in the world, but they have to be able to say why it is the best. (Note that the word *best* is deliberately vague because the aim is for the children to set the criteria of what qualities a dinosaur should possess.)
● Allow time for the children to discuss their ideas about their dinosaurs with their peers as they work on this project. Provide questions for them to think about, such as: *What would the best dinosaur be able to do? What would it look like? How might it behave? What would it eat? How long and where would it live?*
● When the children have made their models, sit them in a circle and ask each child to present their dinosaur with one definition: *My dinosaur is the best sort of dinosaur because…*
● Record the different definitions on a large piece of paper. Encourage the children to say whether they agree or disagree that each definition describes the ideal dinosaur and to explain their answers.
● Through questioning, develop children's thinking and reasoning to determine which traits a dinosaur should have. Is there any one definition of a dinosaur? If not, why not?

Differentiation
For older/more confident learners: Encourage them to use the definitions to match the dinosaur models to themes or concepts such as power, fear and killing.
For younger/less confident learners: Introduce theme cards or labels for each dinosaur to help the children recognise what it is about their dinosaur model that they feel is important.

Talk about it

Hero or zero?

Objective: To listen to each other's views and preferences, agree the next steps to take and identify contributions by each group member.
What you need: Copies of *Tyrannosaurus Drip*, an enlarged copy of photocopiable page 22 and a copy for each child.
Cross-curricular links: PSHE/philosophy.

What to do
● Ask the class to explain the possible meaning of the phrase: *Drip turned from a zero to a hero.*
● Display the enlarged copy of photocopiable page 22 and talk through the scenarios. Allow time for the children to independently think about each one and complete their copy to indicate whether they think Stegosaurus Sam is a 'hero' or a 'zero'.
● Bring the class together. Describe the first scenario and ask the children to move to one of two areas depending on what they ticked.
● Allow the groups a few moments to discuss together why they thought this.
● Encourage the groups to share their reasoning with the whole class. Also encourage oppositional dialogue between the groups if there is disagreement.
● Repeat this for all three scenarios. Review as a class whether there is a consensus on what can be deemed heroic behaviour. Ask: *Is heroism the same as bravery? Is it foolish behaviour? Why are some people heroic and others not?*

Differentiation
For older/more confident learners: Challenge the children to think about real or imagined situations involving heroism.
For younger/less confident learners: Together, make a list of characters from film and TV that are heroes or zeros to develop the children's understanding.

Prehistoric problems

Objective: To explain ideas and processes using imaginative and adventurous vocabulary.
What you need: Copies of *Tyrannosaurus Drip*, paper and drawing materials.
Cross-curricular link: Design and technology.

What to do
● Ask the children to refer back to the story and find the text that tells us that the Tyrannosauruses can't get across the river: *And they muttered, "What a shame that bridges aren't invented yet!"*
● Encourage the children to discuss what things may have been invented in prehistoric times and why.
● Working in small groups, challenge the children to pretend to be prehistoric people and design an invention to overcome the following problems:
  ● **Problem 1:** You are trying to cook fish on the fire, but it keeps raining. What could you invent?
  ● **Problem 2:** You have to get your elderly grandmother up to the top of the mountain, but you have a bad back and cannot carry her.
  ● **Problem 3:** You need to get a message to your mum that you will be late home.
● Encourage the children to think, talk and draw collaboratively to illustrate how the new inventions will work. Ask them questions such as: *What will you call your inventions? How will they work and what materials will you use?* (Don't forget there are no shops yet!)

Differentiation
For older/more confident learners: Encourage them to write simple instructions that explain how to work the new inventions and how they have made them.
For younger/less confident learners: Ask them in groups to discuss the invention they would most like to invent, before they begin the design process.

Talk about it

We're going on a dinosaur hunt

Objective: To tell real and imagined stories using the conventions of familiar story language.
What you need: Copies of *Tyrannosaurus Drip* and copies of photocopiable page 23.
Cross-curricular link: Drama.

What to do

● Ensure that the children are familiar with the story and structure of *We're Going on a Bear Hunt* by Michael Rosen.
● Explain that, instead of a bear, the children are going on a hunt for dinosaurs.
● Hand out copies of photocopiable page 23 and ask the children to fill in some details on the map that will help them. They must think of four places or features (from *Tyrannosaurus Drip* or imaginary) that have to be crossed. They then need to think of a sound to accompany each place or feature on their map.
● Allow time for the children to complete this task, then bring everyone together and share some of their ideas.
● Now choose one hunt at random to act out as a whole class, using language from the Bear Hunt story: *We're going on a dinosaur hunt, we're going to catch a big one, we're not scared… uh oh…* and so on.

Differentiation
For older/more confident learners: Invite them to make their own dinosaur hunter reporter's books written in the past tense: *We went on a hunt and saw…* and so on.
For younger/less confident learners: Ask them to work in small groups to complete an enlarged copy of photocopiable page 23. Then, using a collection of ideas, act out the class dinosaur hunt.

Which came first?

Objective: To use talk to organise, sequence and clarify thinking, ideas, feelings and events.
What you need: Copies of *Tyrannosaurus Drip* and an enlarged copy of photocopiable page 24.
Cross-curricular links: PSHE/philosophy, RE.

What to do

● Talk with the children about how the whole story of *Tyrannosaurus Drip* depends upon the Duckbill egg and where it ends up. Explain that one of the biggest philosophical and scientific questions is: *Which came first? The chicken or the egg?*
● Ask the children to think silently for a minute about this question.
● Arrange the children in a circle and remind them of the listening and talking rules, where only one person must speak at a time and they must give reasons for their thinking.
● Now look together at the enlarged copy of photocopiable page 24 and ask the children to give their ideas about each set of pictures, giving full and reasoned answers.
● It is best to be led by the children in this discussion, but be prepared to deal sensitively with religious and spiritual perspectives that may arise.
● You may want to use the activity as a starting point for a study of different creation myths – Christian, Islamic, Hindu, Inuit, Aboriginal Australian and Native American, for example.

Differentiation
For older/more confident learners: Push for deeper thinking with the use of more challenging questioning. Ask the children for examples and check for logical and consistent thinking.
For younger/less confident learners: Provide them with individual copies of photocopiable page 24 and ask them to highlight which they think came first, giving reasons. Collect in the completed sheets, count which answers have the most votes and discuss why.

Hero or zero?

● Stegosaurus Sam is a friend of Drip's. One day, he was out for a walk and he saw a very fierce Tyrannosaurus Rex stealing a baby Pterodactyl's ice cream. Look at these three different scenarios and decide whether Sam is a 'hero' or a 'zero' in each one.

Hero ☐   **Zero** ☐

Hero ☐   **Zero** ☐

Hero ☐   **Zero** ☐

Illustration © 2010, Andy Keylock/Beehive Illustration.

We're going on a dinosaur hunt

● On the map draw four locations or features that you will see on your hunt, and write the sounds you will hear in the speech bubbles.

Which came first?

● For each pair below, decide which came first.

Chicken | Egg

Mother | Baby

Night | Day

Numbers | Counting

Get writing

From my point of view

> **Objective:** To give some reasons why things happen or characters change.
> **What you need:** Copies of *Tyrannosaurus Drip*, copies of photocopiable page 28 and pencils.
> **Cross-curricular link:** PSHE.

What to do

● After reading the story, ask the children to consider what role the Compsognathus plays. Have they noticed how he starts all the trouble and then watches as the drama unfolds? Which pages can they spot him on?

● Explain to the children that photocopiable page 28 shows a scenario from the story with an empty speech bubble. They must decide what the Compsognathus is saying about what he sees or thinks is happening and write these ideas in the speech bubble.

● Ask the children to think about whether Comp intended to cause all this trouble or whether the events were caused by accident.

● Now think about what could have happened in the story of *Tyrannosaurus Drip* if Comp had done something different with the egg.

● Ask them to think about the consequences of the following alternative events:

  ● The egg hatches and out comes the fiercest dinosaur in the world.
  ● The egg rolls into a nest of tiny insect-sized dinosaurs and hatches.
  ● The egg hatches in a nest of flying dinosaurs.

● In small groups or with a partner, allow the children time to share ideas and suggestions about what might happen. Pose questions such as: *How would the story change? Why would it have to change? Would Drip have to behave differently? What would happen to the other dinosaurs? Would the ending change too?*

> **Differentiation**
> **For older/more confident learners:** Encourage the children to find two other situations in the book that the Compsognathus could comment on.
> **For younger/less confident learners:** Ask the children to explore the situation on the photocopiable page through role play first.

Compare the stories

> **Objective:** To recognise the main elements that shape different texts.
> **What you need:** Copies of *Tyrannosaurus Drip*, 'Cinderella' and 'The Ugly Duckling', copies of photocopiable page 29 and pencils.

What to do

● Read the three stories to the children. Explain that they are going to find comparisons between the two fairy tales and *Tyrannosaurus Drip*.

● Hand out copies of photocopiable page 29 and ask the children to select events from *Tyrannosaurus Drip* that are similar to either of the fairy tales.

● Ask them to write a simple phrase or sentence that illustrates this – for example, *When the egg hatches, one of the dinosaurs is ugly* could be written under the illustration for 'The Ugly Duckling'.

● Allow time for everybody to write a comparison for each heading.

● Now bring the class together and share examples of their comparisons. Which fairy story does *Tyrannosaurus Drip* remind them of most? Encourage them to explain why.

> **Differentiation**
> **For older/more confident learners:** Challenge the children to find more than one example of similar scenarios for each story.
> **For younger/less confident learners:** Allow the children to act out similar scenes from the other stories before they attempt to write them down. Provide a bank of useful words.

Get writing

Explorer's suitcase

> **Objective:** To attempt writing for various purposes, using features of different forms such as lists.
> **What you need:** Copies of photocopiable page 30, writing and drawing materials.
> **Cross-curricular link:** PSHE.

What to do
● Explain to the children that they are going to take on the role of explorers hunting for dinosaurs and they have to pack their suitcases ready to go.
● Allow some thinking and talking time. Ask the children to think about what sort of environments they will encounter. What will the weather be like? What will they need to survive in the environment?

● Hand out copies of photocopiable page 30 and ask each child to write a list of the essential items they will need to take with them. They can add illustrations and write a name and address on the luggage label.
● Share the suggested items and discuss why they will be useful.

> **Differentiation**
> **For older/more confident learners:** Invite the children to write a letter to put in the suitcase, explaining why they are going on this mission and what dangers they may encounter.
> **For younger/less confident learners:** Provide a selection of items that they can write labels for – for example, matches, water bottle, sun cream, insect repellent, binoculars, wellington boots and so on.

Lucky dinosaur dip

> **Objective:** To spell new words using phonics as the prime approach.
> **What you need:** A set of phonics cards, a whiteboard and pens, paper and pencils.

What to do
● Ask the children to tell you any dinosaur names that they know. As you write them on the board, discuss sound combinations and use word-building skills. Talk about how many of them have the same endings.
● Tell the children that they have been given the job of inventing a name for a recently discovered dinosaur.
● Place the letter sounds face down on the floor.
● Ask volunteers to come up to choose a letter sound and place it on the board, saying its sound.

Repeat this until you have nine or ten sounds. Now write the following dinosaur name endings below them: '-osaurus', '-odon', '-ocus'.
● Hand out the paper and pencils and ask the children to write down the sounds at the top of their paper. Challenge them to rearrange the sounds and add one of the name endings to make a new dinosaur name.
● Ask for volunteers to come and write their new words on the board and have fun trying to sound them out.

> **Differentiation**
> **For older/more confident learners:** Add digraphs to the sound cards and encourage the children to add a description of the new breed of dinosaurs.
> **For younger/less confident learners:** Use five sound cards and add this word to another word made from five sounds to help them build new dinosaur names.

Get writing

Dear dinosaur

> **Objective:** To attempt writing for various purposes, using features of different forms.
> **What you need:** Copies of *Tyrannosaurus Drip*, examples of letters written to various people, paper, pencils, envelopes and stamps.
> **Cross-curricular link:** PSHE.

What to do

● After reading the story, tell the children that they must choose a character from the book to write a letter to. Explain that their letter will be offering advice to their chosen dinosaur.

● Share some examples of letters and discuss the format and composition of a letter and how it differs from other forms of writing.

● Discuss together what advice they would give to each dinosaur. For example, could the Compsognathus be told not to steal other people's eggs? Do the Tyrannosaurus sisters need to be told to be kinder to Drip, or does Drip need advice on how to deal with being different?

● Ask the children to write their letters individually. They can then add illustrations and address the envelopes.

● 'Post' the letters in a class post box and select some to read to the class.

> **Differentiation**
> **For older/more confident learners:** Challenge them to write more detailed and complex letters using punctuation and increased phonetic knowledge.
> **For younger/less confident learners:** Allow them to use a writing role-play area with dinosaur name labels and letter writing prompts and equipment.

Dinosaur T

> **Objective:** To convey information and ideas in simple non-narrative forms.
> **What you need:** Copies of *Tyrannosaurus Drip*, a selection of information books and recipe books, paper and pencils.

What to do

● Ask the children to tell you the favourite foods of the Duckbill dinosaurs and the Tyrannosauruses, as they are described in the book – *juicy water weeds* and *Duckbill dinosaurs*.

● Now tell the children that you are opening a restaurant for dinosaurs and need to create an exciting new recipe for each dinosaur. (Explain that they will come in to eat on different days!)

● Allow some time for the class to share recipe books containing vegetarian and meat ideas.

● Challenge the children to write a simple recipe for a meal that each of the two types of dinosaurs may enjoy.

● Encourage them to substitute ingredients for things that might have been found in the dinosaur's environment, such as swamp leaves or mosquito eggs.

> **Differentiation**
> **For older/more confident learners:** Encourage the children to research what animals and plants might have been around during dinosaur times and to include examples of these in their recipes.
> **For younger/less confident learners:** Ask the children to draw their recipe and the ingredients, and write labels to indicate what to use.

From my point of view

- What can the Compsognathus see? What is he thinking?
- Write a sentence or two in the speech bubble.

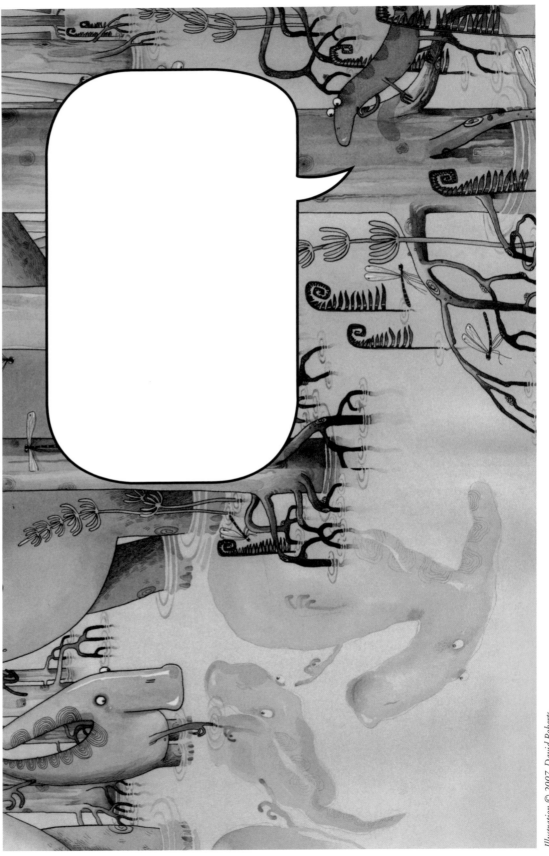

Illustration © 2007, David Roberts.

Compare the stories

● Which parts of *Tyrannosaurus Drip* are similar to these traditional tales? Make notes under the relevant headings.

Cinderella	The Ugly Duckling

It is similar to 'Cinderella' because…	It is similar to 'The Ugly Duckling' because…

Illustration © 2010, Andy Keylock/Beehive Illustration.

Explorer's suitcase

● Make a list of everything you will need to take on your expedition to hunt for dinosaurs.

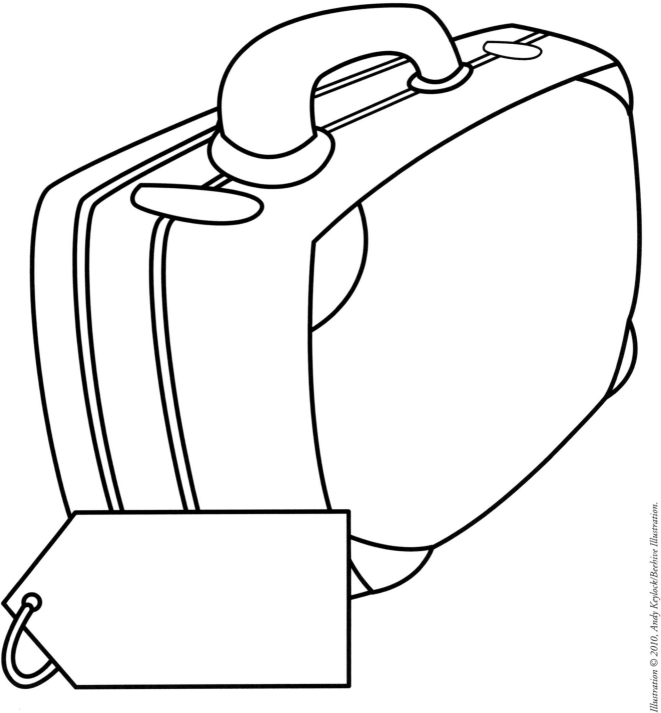

Assessment

Assessment advice

This classic picture book, *Tyrannosaurus Drip*, provides plentiful opportunities for children to explore the playfulness of the spoken word. It allows them to think about the rhyme and rhythm of prose and to develop skills as a critical reader of text, illustration and humorous word play. The children will also enjoy experimenting with the repetition and familiar phrases. This is essentially a read-aloud book, which the children will quickly learn to repeat with gusto!

The learning opportunities juxtapose the humour with lots of historical, scientific and geographical understanding. The activities in this book encourage children to think creatively about issues such as survival, identity and having courage to be yourself. Children will be given opportunities to put themselves in the position of several of the characters, allowing them to empathise and think from alternative points of view.

The nature of the book allows children to engage in a text that brings characters to life through performance skills. They will enjoy the chance to immerse themselves in role play, drama, song and dance activities. This will lead to a better understanding of character, setting and plot, and discussion about all these elements.

Encouraging children to create a game based on this story will provide you with a thorough insight into their understanding of what life was like for the dinosaurs long ago and how we can learn to be better people now.

Across the swamp

> **Assessment focus:** To show understanding of familiar themes and characters through improvisation and role play.
> **What you need:** Copies of *Tyrannosaurus Drip*, enlarged copies of photocopiable page 32, pencils, dice and counters.
> **Cross-curricular links:** Drama, music.

What to do

● Show the class an enlarged copy of photocopiable page 32 and discuss what the children think it might be. Ask: *How could you make it into a game? What ideas do you have to make it exciting?*
● Read the story again to the children and ask them to think about parts of the book that could translate to a game – for example, having to cross the river, looking down at the reflection, Drip running away and so on.
● Talk about what makes a game exciting – for example, moving on extra squares, doing a forfeit, missing a go, picking up a bonus, moving up a ladder or down a snake and so on.
● Hand out enlarged copies of photocopiable page 32 and ask the children to design their own board games, thinking about what elements they can build into the game that reflect the events of the story.
● Ask children to colour in their games and add scenery around the track.
● Allow opportunities for the children to create counters for the game based on characters from the story. These could be made from clay or card mounted in Blu-Tack®.
● Have fun sharing and playing the games and add them to display work done on this book.

Across the swamp

● Add your own details and decorate this board to make it into an exciting *Tyrannosaurus Drip* game!

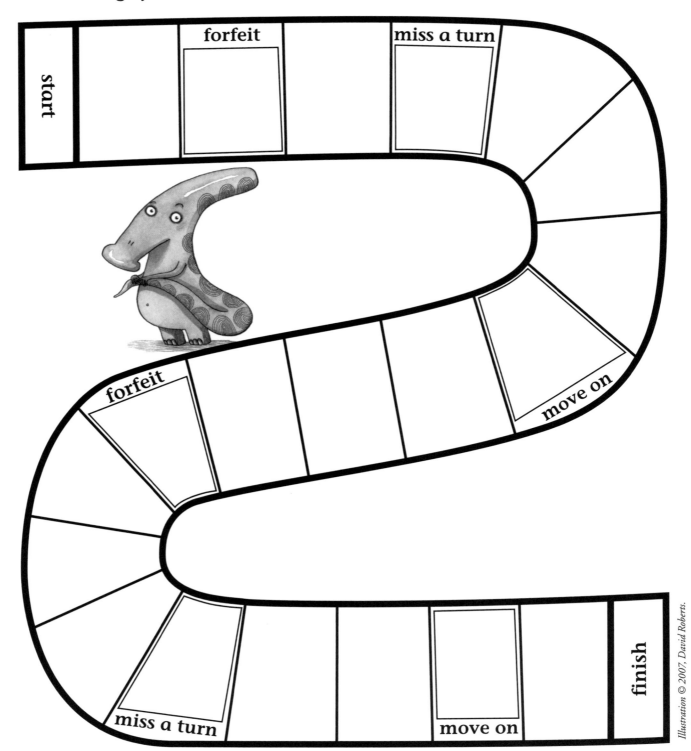

start

forfeit

miss a turn

forfeit

move on

miss a turn

move on

finish

Illustration © 2007, David Roberts.